Make

Troubl e

Make Trouble

JOHN WATERS

Illustrated by Eric Hanson

corsair

CORSAIR
First published in the US in 2017 by Algonquin
First published in Great Britain in 2017 by Corsair

1 3 5 7 9 10 8 6 4 2

Grunge art, pages 34-35 © Thoth Adan, istockphoto.com
Author photo © Stephen Maturen, Illustrations © Eric Hanson, Art direction and design by Anne C. Winslow

A CIP catalogue record for this book is available from the British Library.

ISBN: 978-1-4721-5329-6

Printed in Italy

Papers used by Corsair are from well-managed forests and other responsible sources.

Corsair
An imprint of
Little, Brown Book Group
Carmelite House
50 Victoria Embankment
London EC4Y 0DZ

An Hachette UK Company
www.hachette.co.uk

www.littlebrown.co.uk

Make
Trouble

John Waters

was invited to address

a recent graduating class

of the

Rhode Island School of Design.

This is his speech.

I should say right off that I am really qualified to be your commencement speaker.

I was suspended from high school, then kicked out of college in the first marijuana scandal ever on a university campus. I've been arrested several times.

I've been known
to dress in ludicrous
fashions. I've also
built a career out of
negative reviews,
and have been called
the Prince of Puke
by the press.

And most recently a title I'm really proud of:

The People's
Pervert

I am honored
to be here today
with my people.

Okay,

I'M SUPPOSED TO

INSPIRE YOU.

HOW'S THIS?

Somehow I've been able to
make a living doing what I love best
for fifty years without ever having
to get a real job.

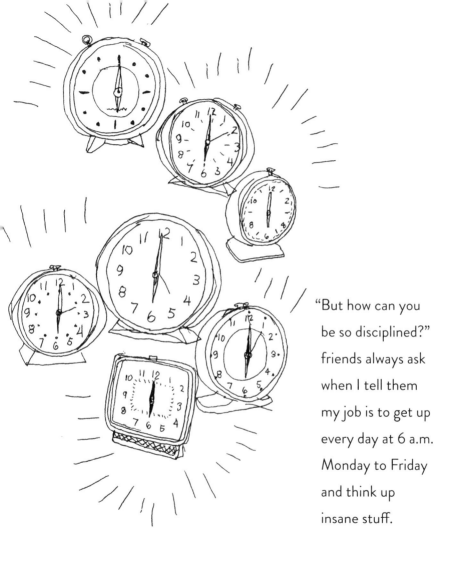

"But how can you be so disciplined?" friends always ask when I tell them my job is to get up every day at 6 a.m. Monday to Friday and think up insane stuff.

Easy! If I didn't work
this hard for myself,
I'd have to go work
for somebody else.
Plus, I can go to my
office one room away
from my bedroom
in my own house
dressed in my
underpants
if I want to.

You're lucky.

When I went to school,
my teachers discouraged
every dream I ever had.
I wanted to be the filthiest
person alive, but no school
would let me. Today, you
could possibly even make
a snuff movie in college
and get an A+.

Hopefully you have been taught
never to fear rejection in the workplace.

Remember, a "no" is free.

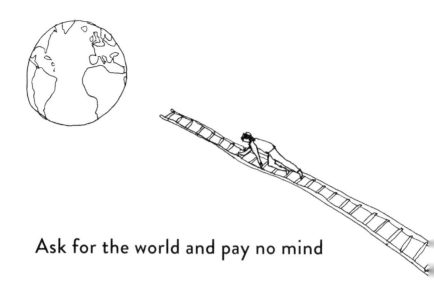

Ask for the world and pay no mind

if you are initially turned down.

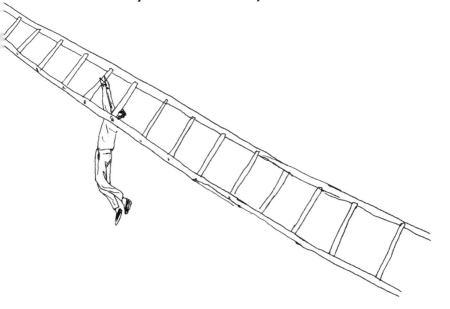

A career in the arts is like a hitchhiking trip: All you need is one person to say "get in," and off you go.

THERE

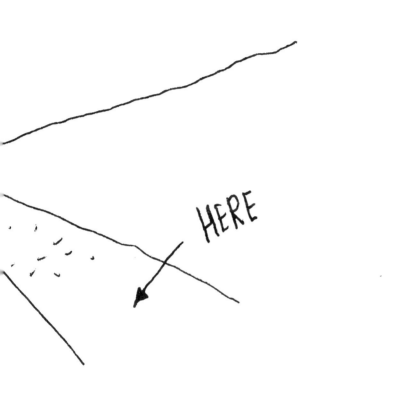

HERE

And then the confidence begins.

Of course,
play is equally
as important to
your education
as work.

And in the fine arts, play *is* work, isn't it?

What other field allows you to deduct as business expenses from your taxes gangsta rap, Gaspar Noé's movies, even vintage porn as long as you use it for research?

REMEMBER: you must participate in the creative world you want to become part of.

SO WHAT IF YOU HAVE TALENT?

THEN WHAT?

You have to
figure out how to
work your way inside.
Keep up with what's
causing chaos
in your own field.

If you're a visual artist, go see the shows in the galleries that are frantically competing to find the one bad neighborhood left in Manhattan to open up in.

Watch every movie that gets a negative review in the *New York Times* and figure out what the director did wrong. Or right!

Read, read, read!

Watch people on the streets.

SPY,

BE NOSY,

EAVESDROP.

nd, as you get older, you'll need youth spies that will keep you abreast of new music that nobody your age has heard of yet or body-piercing mutilations that are becoming all the rage—even budding sexually transmitted diseases you should go to any length to avoid.

ever be like some of my generation who say, "We had more fun in the sixties." No, we didn't! The kids today who still live with their parents (who haven't seen them in months but leave food outside their bedroom doors) are having just as much fun shutting down the governments of foreign countries on their computer as we did banning the bomb.

Today may be the end of

your juvenile delinquency,

but it should also be the

first day of your new adult

disobedience.

THESE DAYS,
EVERYBODY WANTS
TO BE

AN OUTSIDER,

POLITICALLY CORRECT
TO A FAULT.

hat's good. I hope you *are* working to end racism, sexism, ageism, fatism. But is that enough? Isn't being an outsider sooo last year? I mean, maybe it's time to throw caution to the wind, *really* shake things up, and reinvent yourself as a new version of your most dreaded enemy:

Like I am.

The final irony—
a creatively crazy person
who finally gets power.

**Think about it:
I didn't change.
Society did.**

Who would have
ever thought a top
college would invite
a filth elder like myself
to set an example
to its students?

See? There's hope for everybody.

You need
to prepare
sneak attacks
on society.

Hairspray is the only really devious movie
I ever made. The musical based on it is now being
performed in practically every high school in
America—and nobody seems to notice it's a show
with two men singing a love song to each other that
also encourages white teen girls to date black guys.
Pink Flamingos was preaching to the converted.

But *Hairspray* is a Trojan horse: it snuck into
Middle America and never got caught.
You can do the same thing.

Listen to your political enemies, especially the smart ones, and then figure out a way to make them laugh.

SPEECH
ALARM

Nobody likes a bore on a soapbox.

Humor is always the best defense *and* weapon. If you can make an idiot laugh, they'll at least pause and listen before they do something stupid . . . to you.

Refuse to isolate yourself. Separatism is for losers.

Gay is not enough anymore. It's a good
start, but I don't want my memoirs to be in
the gay section near true crime at the back
of the bookstore next to the bathrooms.
No! I want it up front with the best sellers.
And don't heterosexual kids actually receive
more prejudice in art schools today than
the gay ones? Things are a-changing.
It's a confusing time.

T R I G G E R

|||||||||||||||||||||||||||||||||||||||||||||||||||||||||||||||||||||||||

This might be time for a trigger warning—
the amazing concept I've heard about in which
you're supposed to warn students if you're
going to talk about something that challenges
their values. I thought that's why you *went*
to college. My whole life has been a trigger
warning. But you have been warned. So the
trigger warning is in effect, and now back to
the prepared speech.

|||||||||||||||||||||||||||||||||||||||||||||||||||||||||||||||||||||||||

W A R N I N G

Don't hate all rich people. They're not all awful.

Believe me, I know some evil poor people, too.

I'm rich! I don't mean money-wise. I mean that
I have figured out how to never be around assholes
at any time in my personal and professional life.
That's rich.

It's okay to hate the poor, too,
but only the poor of spirit,
not wealth.

A poor person to me can
have a big bank balance,
but is uncurious, judgmental,
isolated, and unavailable
to change.

I'm also sorry
to report there's
no such thing
as karma.

So many of my talented,
great friends are dead
and so many of the fools
I've met and loathed are
still alive. It's not fair,
and it never will be.

Parents, now it's time
to talk to you.

od, these kids can be brats, can't they? Entitled little bastards. Do they think you're made of money? Can't they give you a second to adjust to such social changes as sexual reassignment surgery, horn implants, and the political rights of the adult-baby community?

AND, YOUNG ADULTS,

MAYBE TODAY IS THE DAY YOU

STOP

BLAMING YOUR PARENTS

FOR EVERY PROBLEM YOU'VE

EVER HAD.

Whining is never appealing
in a college graduate.

Yes, it's a drag you were kept locked in a cardboard box
under their bed and whipped daily with a car aerial,
but it's time to move on. We've all been dealt a hand.
Deal with it!

And, parents, vice versa:
You don't get to order up your kids,
either.

Maybe your daughter did tattoo
her entire face.
Well, work with what you got!
Think positively:
maybe she'll open a fancy tattoo
parlor in Paris.

I'm touched to sometimes see distraught parents bringing their angry and defiant teenage children with them to see my spoken-word show in a last-ditch effort to bond. At least both sides are trying.

The truce
of maturity will
come to families
if every member
is patient.

I often look back in wonder at how understanding my parents were. Dr. Spock didn't have a chapter in his child-rearing book on how to handle your son if all he wanted to do as a child was play "car accident." Yet my mom took me to junkyards as a toddler and let me wander around fantasizing ghoulishly.

My dad even lent me the money to make *Pink Flamingos*, and I paid him back in full—with interest. But, looking back, did I really expect him to be thrilled that I had made one of the "most vile, stupid, and repulsive films ever made," as *Variety* called it?

My parents
made me feel safe,
and that's why
I'm up here today.

That's what you should try to do
for your kids, too—no matter *where* you
get your children these days.

CONTEMPORARY ART'S JOB IS TO

WORK

WHAT CAME BEFORE.

Is there a better job description than that to aspire to?

Here's another

TRIGGER
WARNING

and pardon me for swearing:

Go out
in the world
and fuck it up
beautifully.

DESIGN

clothes so hideous that they
can't be worn ironically.

HORRIFY

us with new ideas.

OUTRAGE

outdated critics.

USE
TECHNOLOGY

for transgression, not lazy social living.

MAKE ME

NERVOUS!

AND FINALLY,

COUNT YOUR
BLESSINGS.

You got through college. You didn't commit suicide,
OD, or have a nervous breakdown, and let's remember
the ones who did.

IT'S TIME TO

get

busy.

It's your turn

to

make

trouble.

BUT THIS TIME
IN THE REAL WORLD.
AND THIS TIME FROM
THE INSIDE.

Thank you very much.

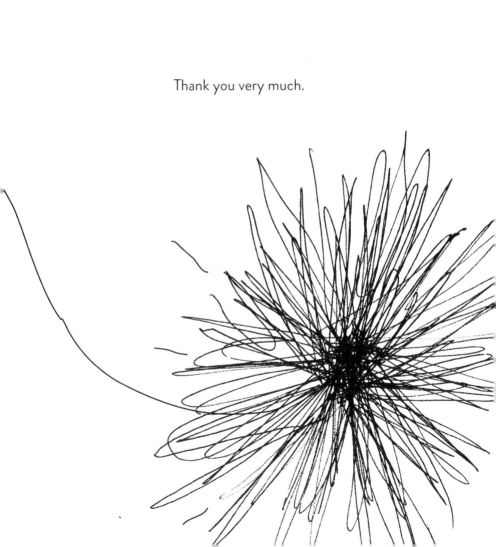

JOHN WATERS is a filmmaker, writer, actor, and visual artist best known for the films *Pink Flamingos*, *Serial Mom*, and *Hairspray*, which was adapted into a long-running Broadway musical. The author of seven books, among them the *New York Times* bestsellers *Carsick* and *Role Models*, he performs his one-man, spoken-word shows regularly.

Waters lives in Baltimore, Maryland.